TO: _Allyn, on your 2nd_
birthday ❀

For God so loved the world
that he gave his one and
only Son, that whoever
believes in him shall not
perish but have eternal life.

John 3:16, NIV

WITH LOVE:
~~FROM:~~ _Aunt Jennifer_

God's Love for Little Ones
Copyright ©1995
by the Zondervan Corporation

ISBN 0-310-97172-1

Project Editor: Jesslyn DeBoer
Design: Anne Huizenga
Illustrations: Comark Group
Layout: Mark Veldheer

Made in the United States of America
98 99 00 / Q / 10 9 8 7 6 5 4

GOD'S LOVE FOR
LITTLE ONES

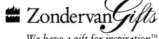

Zondervan*Gifts*

We have a gift for inspiration™

God tells us of his love in
these stories from the Bible:

Creation
Noah
Baby Moses
Miriam
Ruth
Daniel
Baby Jesus
A Little Girl
Zacchaeus
The Little Children
The Living Jesus
All People

CREATION

In the beginning
there was nothing.

Then God made the
sky and the earth.

God made the sun
and the stars.

God made the water.

God made the land.

He made the fish
and the birds and all
the animals.

God made people
too.

He put them on the
earth.

God loves his world.

NOAH

Noah was God's friend.

He listened to God.

God told Noah to
build a big boat.

Noah put his family
in the boat.

He put many
animals in it too.

Then it rained and
rained and rained.
It rained for
forty days.

Noah and his family
and the animals
were safe inside
the boat.

God sent a
rainbow to show
them his love.

God loved Noah
and his family.

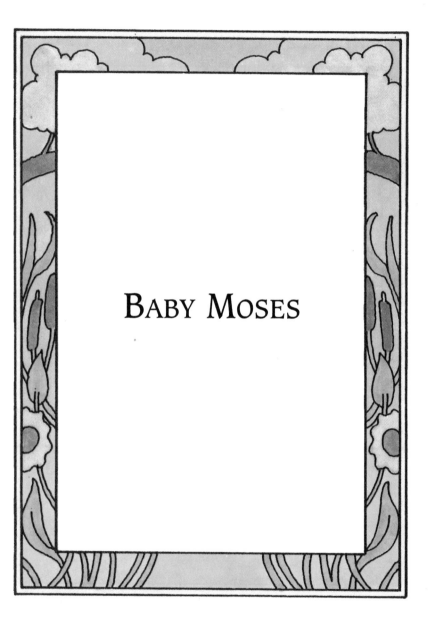

BABY MOSES

Moses was a strong, beautiful baby.

His mother hid him
from the soldiers
who were killing the
Hebrew baby boys.

She put baby Moses
in a basket and
placed it in the river.

A princess found
Moses in the basket.

The princess kept
baby Moses safe
from the soldiers.

God loved baby
Moses.

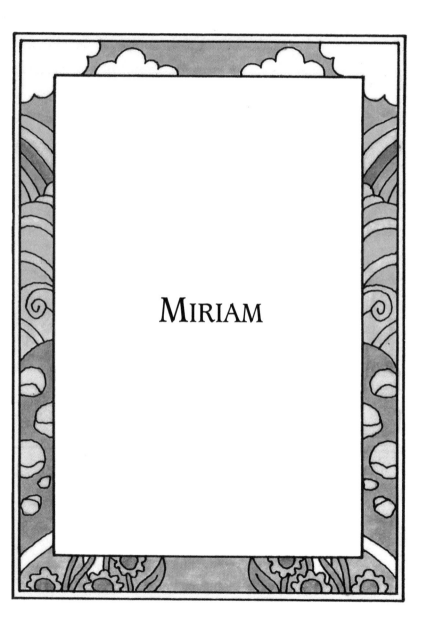

MIRIAM

Miriam was
Moses' sister.

They lived with
God's special people
in Egypt.

The king of Egypt
was very mean to
God's people.

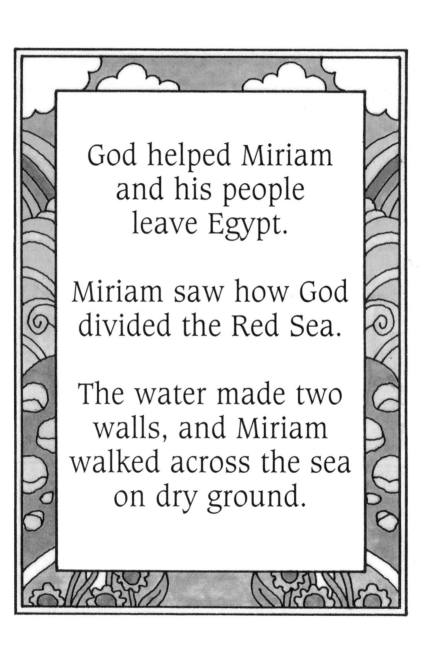

God helped Miriam
and his people
leave Egypt.

Miriam saw how God
divided the Red Sea.

The water made two
walls, and Miriam
walked across the sea
on dry ground.

When Miriam reached the other shore, she danced and sang a special song of thanks to God.

God loved Miriam.

RUTH

Ruth was sad.

Her husband
had died.

She had no
children . . .

but she loved her husband's mother, Naomi.

Ruth promised to always stay with Naomi.

She promised to love Naomi's God and Naomi's people.

God blessed Ruth.
He gave her a
new husband and
a baby boy.

God loved Ruth.

DANIEL

Every day Daniel prayed to God.

One day the king said, "No one may pray to God."

But Daniel prayed anyway.

The king told the
soldiers to throw
Daniel into a
den of lions.

But God kept
Daniel safe.

The lions did not
hurt him.

Daniel trusted God
and obeyed him.

God loved Daniel.

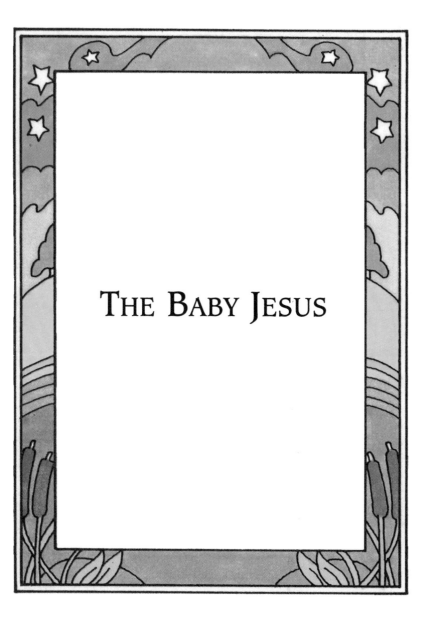

THE BABY JESUS

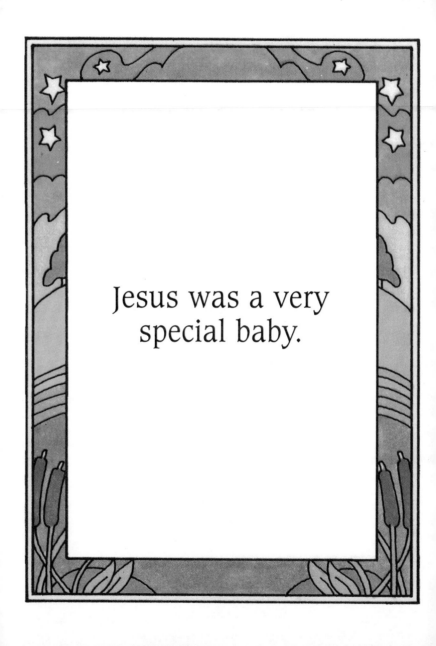

Jesus was a very
special baby.

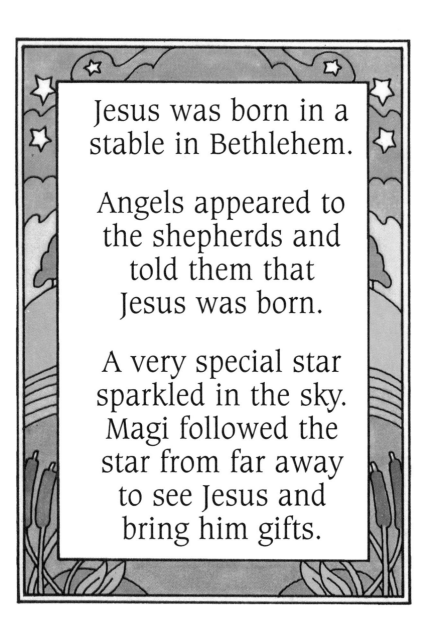

Jesus was born in a
stable in Bethlehem.

Angels appeared to
the shepherds and
told them that
Jesus was born.

A very special star
sparkled in the sky.
Magi followed the
star from far away
to see Jesus and
bring him gifts.

Jesus was the
Son of God.

God loved the
baby Jesus.

A LITTLE GIRL

When Jesus was a grown man, he helped many people.

Once a little girl was very sick. Her father went to Jesus for help. Jesus came to their house. Everyone was crying because the little girl was dead.

Then Jesus did something wonderful!

Jesus took the little
girl by the hand
and made her
alive again!

God loved the
little girl.

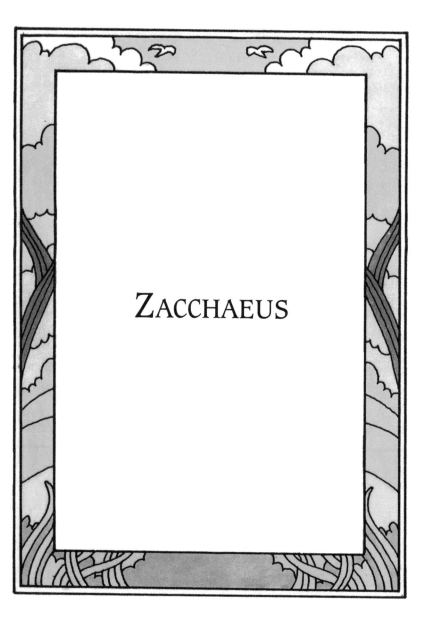

ZACCHAEUS

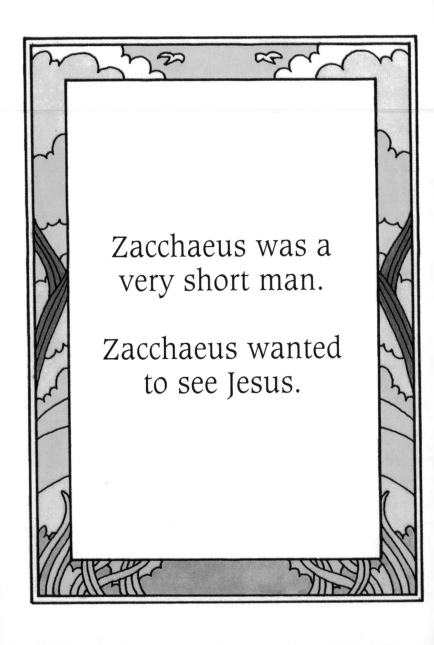

Zacchaeus was a
very short man.

Zacchaeus wanted
to see Jesus.

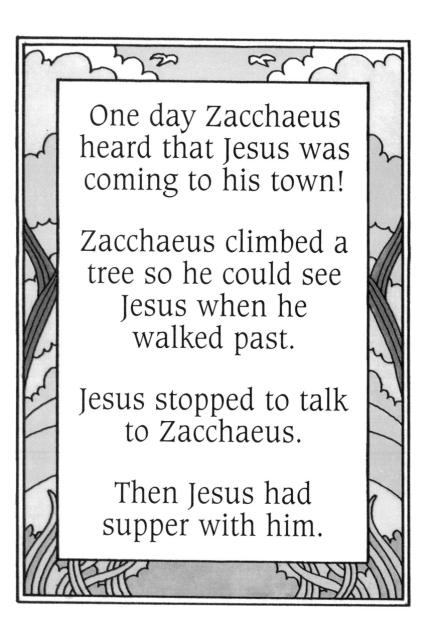

One day Zacchaeus heard that Jesus was coming to his town!

Zacchaeus climbed a tree so he could see Jesus when he walked past.

Jesus stopped to talk to Zacchaeus.

Then Jesus had supper with him.

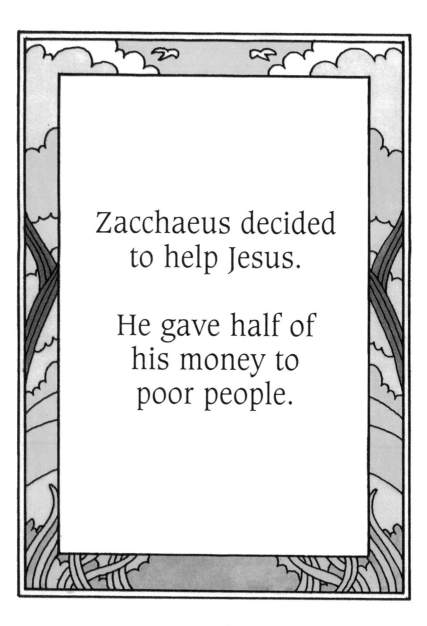

Zaccheaus decided
to help Jesus.

He gave half of
his money to
poor people.

God loved
Zacchaeus.

THE LITTLE
CHILDREN

Some people
brought their children
to see Jesus.

They wanted Jesus
to touch their
children and to pray
for them.

The little children
were very special
to Jesus.

Jesus said, "Let the little children come to me."

Jesus talked to the children.

He gave them hugs!

God loved the little children.

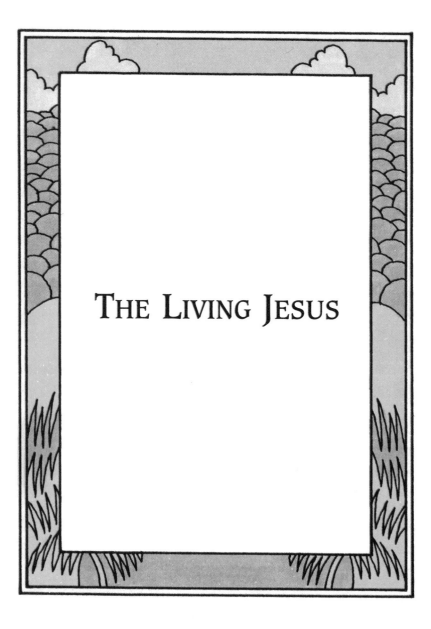

THE LIVING JESUS

Jesus knew he
had to die.

He knew God sent
him to earth to die
for everyone's sins.

Many people didn't
like Jesus.

They cheered when
the rulers chose
to kill Jesus.

But Jesus did not
stay dead.

He came out of his
grave in three days,
just like he said
he would!

One day Jesus went
up into heaven.

Angels told his disciples that Jesus would come to earth again!

God loved
His Son Jesus.

ALL PEOPLE

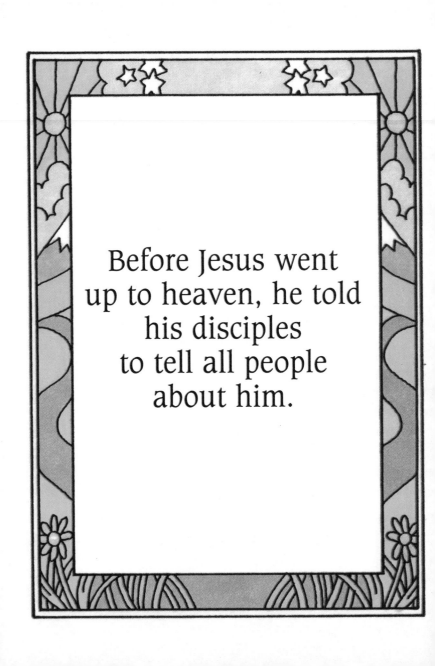

Before Jesus went
up to heaven, he told
his disciples
to tell all people
about him.

God loves tall people
and short people.

God loves big people
and small.

God loves all the
people in his world.

God loves you!

And God wants you
to love him, too!